For Barnaby

First published 1983 by Walker Books Ltd
87 Vauxhall Walk, London SE11 5HJ

This edition published 2013

2 4 6 8 10 9 7 5 3 1

© 1983 Helen Oxenbury

This book has been typeset in Veronan light

Printed in China

British Library Cataloguing in Publication Data:
a catalogue record for this book is available from the British Library

ISBN 978-1-4063-4147-8

www.walker.co.uk

The Birthday Party

Helen Oxenbury

WALKER BOOKS
AND SUBSIDIARIES
LONDON · BOSTON · SYDNEY · AUCKLAND

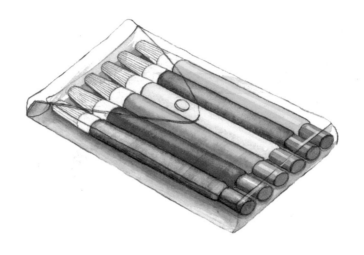

I chose John's birthday
present on my own.

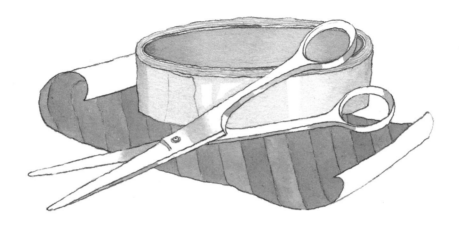

"Can't I try them out, Mum?"
"No," Mum said, "we bought
them for John."

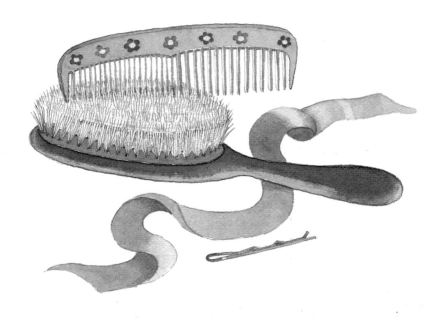

"Let's have your blue ribbon
as well," Mum said.

"Is that my present?"
John said when we arrived.

"Happy birthday, John," Mum said.
She made me give him the present.

"Here's my cake," John shouted.
He just left my present
on the floor.

After tea we had games and
balloons and running about
and jumping and bumping.

My dad collected me.
"Give her the balloon,"
John's mum said.
"Do you really want it?" John said.
"Yes please," I said. "I do."

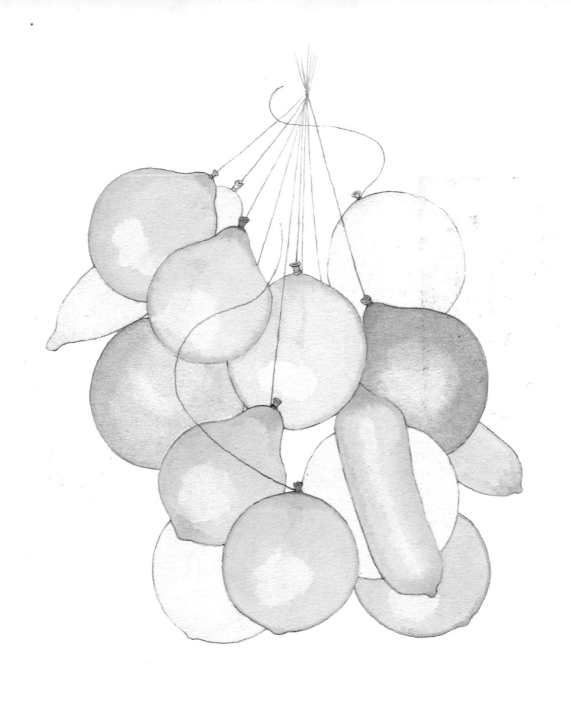